Blackbird Fly! A Mother's Story of Grief, Love and Hope

A mother's story of grief, love and hope

D1509128

Judy Beene Myers

dedication:
To Trey
"all your life you were only waiting for this moment to arise."

introduction:

"You are going to have to give and give and give, or there's no reason for you to be writing. You have to give from the deepest part of yourself, and you are going to have to go on giving and the giving is going to have to be its own reward. There is no cosmic importance to your getting something published, but there is learning to be a giver."

—Ann Lamott

I did not plan to write this. The reality is this writing wrote me. Eight months following my son's unexpected and sudden death I was invited by a friend to participate in a writing group. I do not know why I agreed. I was still very much in what I have come to know as a "non-ordinary" state, not fully aware most of the time what I was doing and undecided from one moment to the next as to what I could allow myself to participate in.

I have always been a writer, of sorts. I majored in journalism and worked for a few years as a staff writer for a metropolitan newspaper. I have written quite a lot through the years, primarily for family and friends. It has always felt to me to be the most natural and comfortable means of in-depth communication.

The writing group began with classes taught by Elizabeth Harper Neeld. I knew that many years ago she had experienced the unexpected loss of her husband who collapsed and died while jogging. Her book, SEVEN CHOICES, Finding Daylight After Loss Shatters Your World, was one of the first books I read after my son's death. Had the class been taught by anyone else, I am not certain I would have attended. I also knew that there would be at least three people in the group I felt comfortable with, who knew me and who were aware of my recent loss. I decided to at least try the class and see where it led me.

After a series of three sessions taught by Elizabeth, we began to meet as a group twice monthly to share our writing and hear that of others in the group. Following each writer's presentation, members of the group answered simple questions based on what we heard the writer convey.

For the fist six months I simply showed up. I wrote some but certainly did not read. During that time, I asked Elizabeth to meet with me. It is difficult to explain how foreign one feels in the early stages of traumatic loss. I wanted to be sure she knew what had happened. I wanted to know if other members of the group, those I did not know previously, were aware of this tragedy. Times of deep grief can lead one into total confusion and distrust. I felt I had no place, that I did not belong.

At the first class Elizabeth said, "Declare you have a writing project." One day completely spontaneously I said to my family, "I have a writing project I am working on." Eventually I branched out and made that declarative statement to a few friends. I am a person of my word. How could I declare a writing project and not take action? So I began by just writing something. I believe I actually tried to avoid writing what wanted to be written. Elizabeth also said, "Just do something every day," so I did even if was just putting one photograph in a box or copying a quote.

Finally something opened up in me. I began to do what Ann Lamott said, I began to give and then to give more and more until I began to give from the deepest part of me. The giving became its own reward because it happened that as I gave more, more came forth for me to give. It began to become a gift to myself, to the life of my son, to all who have loved and supported me. It is my offering to anyone who might somehow find it helpful in experiencing any form of grief.

After one of my first readings, a member of the writing group asked me, "How are you doing this?" referring to living with my son's sudden death. I remember thinking at the time: "I really don't know. I am not doing it. Something greater than myself is doing it for me."

I have read about resiliency in recovery from trauma. Much information points to a positive outlook, optimism, making a decision to move forward in life in spite of everything. However, for me I simply began by practicing the principles of my spiritual program which has at its foundation the 12 Steps of Alcoholics Anonymous. These steps gratefully have guided me in sobriety for more than 26 years.

Initially during those early morning hours after learning of my son's death, I reached out for help from those I knew had the spiritual maturity and wisdom to guide me. That is what I did when I came into AA. I admitted I needed help and I sought it.

Automatically after learning of Trey's death, I began to practice the first three steps of AA: I admitted my powerlessness over this situation. I came to believe that in this event as in my alcoholism a power greater than myself could restore me to sanity and I turned my life and my will over to the care of the God of my understanding. The Twelve Steps are the only way that work for me in turning toward any life situation.

In addition I am fortunate to be an active part of Appamada, a Zen Buddhist Sangha in the tradition of American Zen teacher, Joko Beck, led by Peg Syverson and Flint Sparks. Flint is a licensed psychologist and an ordained Zen Buddhist Priest. Peg, a professor of Rhetoric and Writing at the University of Texas, has practiced Zen since the 1960s and has been ordained as a Soto Zen Priest. I regularly sit in Zazen

(Zen meditation) at Appamada and seek the guidance of my teachers. I am held by the close community of Sangha members. Appamada is my place of refuge, solace and peace.

Prior to this tragedy I was introduced to My Healing Place, a nonprofit grief support center here in Austin. The center was started five years ago by Khris Ford, a licensed professional counselor and spiritual director. Khris experienced the loss of her 16-year-old son when he was killed in an automobile accident. I continue to receive support and guidance there and currently serve as a facilitator for grief groups, particularly those serving children.

Now I would answer the question of how I live with this loss by saying: I live on a daily basis connected to those who guide, hold, support and love me. I have many, many people to thank for this. I am deeply grateful for each of them in my life. With regard to my "writing project," my gratitude in making this offering to others experiencing grief is beyond words.

First, I thank you, Elizabeth, for introducing me to a method of writing that speaks to my heart and allowed it to open and say what it so wanted to say. I thank you, Jolynn, for initiating the writing group which now, as we all know, is much more than a writing group. A bow to Sharon for offering a regular place for us to meet; to Margaret for keeping us on track with the guiding questions we are all now very familiar with but continue to want stated for us; to Kat for connecting with me and allowing me to become part of her story; to John for sharing and introducing us all to Cowbird; to Lee and Jen for their stories, humor and quiet gentleness and to Stacey, the one I most feared and the one who turned it all around for me and validated what I already know: we never know each other until we know each other's stories. After all, that is all we are: our stories.

Alice Walker writes about facing the things that scare us. In writing my way through my grief, I have faced many things I have feared, including my own mortality. In many ways this project has relieved me of those fears and opened my heart to what compassion or "suffering with" truly is. I have been changed by giving of myself through writing. I have been able to integrate this grief into my life, to experience in a deeper way the grief of others and to acknowledge that we humans, the highest form of consciousness on this planet of an interconnected system of life, all grieve individually and collectively. I have grieved with other parents who have lost children, with children who have lost a parent or parents, with husbands and wives who have lost a spouse, with grandparents who have lost children and grandchildren.

It is my hope that my writing project will help others turn toward grief and allow it to become transformative as mine has and continues to become. I hope that individually and globally we can face the things that scare us rather than "numbing" ourselves as Joanna Macy calls it in her book, *Coming Back to Life, Practices to Reconnect Our Lives and Our World.*"

She writes that, "When we're distracted and fearful, and the odds are running against us, it is easy to let the heart and mind go numb——of all the dangers we face, from climatic change to nuclear wars, none is so great as the deadening of our response." We cannot deaden our response to grief and live fully.

We cannot deny our grief and expect it to go away; not our individual grief, not the grief of friends and loved ones and not the grief of the world.

"To be conscious in our world today is to be aware of vast suffering and unprecedented peril," says Macy.

My writing is my offering to anyone who grieves. We each experience grief in different ways. Still, we share the same underlying fears, the isolation, the hopelessness, the shattered-ness. If this offering in any way makes a difference for anyone experiencing any kind of grief, then perhaps I am making the difference we each have the opportunity to make when we honor our connectedness.

As Jonathan Safran Foer wrote in *Extremely Loud & Incredibly Close,*

"I asked if he [Dad] could think of a solution to—-'The problem of how relatively insignificant we are.'" He said, 'Well, what would happen if a plane dropped you in the middle of the Sara Desert and picked up a single grain of sand with tweezers and moved it one millimeter?—-What would that mean? Think about it.'

'—-I guess I would have moved one grain of sand.'

'—-which would mean?'

'—-If you hadn't done it, human history would have been one way.'

'—-But you did, so...'

I stood on the bed, pointed my fingers at the fake stars, and screamed:

'—-I changed the course of human history!—that's right.'

'—-I changed the universe.'

'—-You did'"

We never know how far reaching our stories might be or how the simple task of telling them is capable of changing everything: changing the course of history, changing the planet, changing the universe. I have found that a heart broken with grief immense enough to fully break it open is left with a vast capacity for joy: a joy that is able to walk hand in hand with grief, a joy sufficient to encompass and offer healing to all wounds. In discovering this joy we are each capable of healing the wounds of the world and finding that which we all truly seek: peace—-a peace that passes all understanding; peace for

this ever-expanding, wondrous and unending universe, simple and everlasting,
peace.

—-With boundless and endless gratitude,

Judy Beene Myers

I

"One day can bend your life."

—Mitch Albom

"When he stopped breathing the world stopped, and didn't stop. I knelt beside the empty body and a huge impersonal emptiness poured into me and exploded."
—Father Laurence Freeman

It is now more than a year since our Australian Shepherd dog, Timber, barked, ran frantically back and fourth from the front door, up the stairs to our bedroom and back again, startled by someone knocking at 2:30 a.m. Christmas morning. Abruptly awakened, I drowsily hurried to the door. I could see my daughter standing outside in the darkness.

"What's wrong?" I asked as I opened the door. I remember thinking something must have happened at her house, but then if something was wrong there, she would not be here.

"I have something to tell you," she said as she entered, "and it is bad." She sat down on the couch. I sat in a chair facing her.

She motioned me to sit near her. I moved to the couch and sat beside her. I do not remember the sequence of her words. It was something like:

"Dad called—-they have been trying to call you—-Trey, [my 40-year-old son], must have gotten sick—-Amy, [my daughter-in-law], got up and went into the bathroom. Trey had collapsed. They tried to revive him. He is dead."

"No, no, no!" I screamed, shaking my head, "No, not Trey! Not my boy!""

My life from that moment and for many months afterwards became a disconnected blur. The flow of events seemed swept up into a river of broken-heartedness. We woke my husband with the news. I remember trying to think coherently but not being able to. Nothing made sense. This was not supposed to happen. All I could do was feel. All I could feel was emptiness, despair, loss of hope, a deep extinguishing of life itself. It was not only the end of my son's life here and now, it was the end of my life as I had known it.

I remember saying repeatedly through the rush of tears, "I don't know how to do this." I remember feeling I could not get my breath as I sobbed inconsolably, my head in the lap of my good friend, Patty, who arrived immediately after receiving a phone with the news. In the background I somehow knew my daughter and husband were trying to make some plan for what we should do next.

In those early morning hours before leaving for Brownsville where Trey was to spend Christmas with his wife and two small children, I managed to go to the computer and email my spiritual teacher and friend. In an act of total desperation I threw out my lifeline. "You can do this and we are all here to hold and support you," was his reply. "You do not have to do this alone."

As I read those words I sensed through overwhelming grief that I would be able, one tiny moment at a time, to face this unexpected loss in my life. I knew with certainty I was being held by something much greater than myself.

Most of Christmas Day was spent driving to Brownsville. Carroll, my daughter, drove. I remember very little of the trip. There were long periods of silence. I had no sense of minutes or hours. I seemed to be in a state of timelessness. At some point Carroll turned to me and said, "It must have been Trey's time." I yelled back at her in anger and sorrow, "Don't say that! It was not his time! It was not Trey's time!"

Trey's dad, from whom I have been divorced for many years, and wife had earlier arrived in Brownsville from Dallas. I was grateful we had all remained good friends through the years. As we neared our destination I called him and he assured me he would be waiting in front of the house for us. He was. I rushed into his arms, this father of my child, this man who had lost his only son. There were no words. There are no words in moments such as these. There is only connection. There is only holding.

The shock of such a traumatic event is indescribable. I cannot recall how we navigated through Christmas Day nor do I clearly remember the events of the following week which included two family memorial services for Trey, both led by his father and me and both held at sunset on the Padre Island Beach.

Somehow the right words came to us to say, the right people arrived to comfort us at this place where we had spent many summer vacations with our children. Trey had walked the beach there Christmas Eve with his own young children. They filled his baseball cap with shells. He took pictures of himself making funny faces for them. These spontaneous, childlike moments were so like him. I often participated with him in such ridiculousness, both of us with twinkles in our eyes! I know as only a mother knows what those moments with his children meant to him: how deeply he loved them both, how he loved the ocean, the side-stepping crabs, the gulls, the sounds of the surf and jumping the waves.

On December 26, 2010 Trey's dad and stepmother, my husband Ed and I, my daughter, Carroll, daughter-in-law, Amy, my two precious grandchildren, Alice Elizabeth, then 2, and Ty, 1, joined other family members and a few close friends to pay tribute to my son at sunset on the beach. The western sky blazed with the glory of a deep orange and red sunset. I included in what I said that evening words I remembered from a sermon give at the church where my children were raised, "deeply loving another requires our greatest courage because one way or another either I will stand at the grave of a beloved or a beloved will stand at my grave."

When I first heard those words which have remained with me through the years, I imagined losing my mother or my husband or close friends. I never went beyond those imaginings. I certainly never thought of standing at the grave of one of my children. Now I am deeply aware that we never know what love will require of us—-ever. I do know that we must love no matter what the price. We were created by love itself, simply to love and to be loved.

As I spoke that evening surrounded by family and friends, I told them and reminded myself that I have discovered in my life the greatest tragedies, disappointments and challenges, as difficult and painful as they were at the time, have eventually held a blessing if I have allowed myself to turn toward the light.

Little did I know what it would be like to live the words I was saying. The greatest difficulty of turning toward my life now was just beginning. Sometime during that week one of my teachers called, and as I sat under a tree on the island, I listened to her words of comfort and challenge, "Allowing yourself all the time possible in silence will be the most healing thing you can do."

In the painful, awful but also comforting peace of the silence of meditation I have usually been surrounded and held by the presence of others. Other times I have sat alone in solitude. Slowly I have been able to face this death and this unwanted new beginning and slowly I have become and continue to become integrated once more back into the reality of my life.

At sunset on New Years Day, 2011, following a second family service, Amy and I carrying Trey's ashes, waded together into the ocean until knee deep in the surf. I remember hesitating, turning to my husband and softly saying, "I can't do this." He whispered, "Yes, you can." I turned toward Amy and together we released Trey to the sea in the presence of loved ones to sounds of night winds ushering the tide ashore beneath a bright starlit, full moon sky. In my stunned and wandering mind I heard the words of Ash Wednesday. "Oh, man, dust thou art, to dust thou shall return."

Now, as I write this, more than a year has passed since Trey's death. My daily intent is to allow this unwanted circumstance to weave itself into the ever-emerging pattern of my life. I want another word for death. I am angered that there seem to be no appropriate words for this moving on. The word death in our Western culture seems so final. I do not and cannot believe it is. Instead, I believe it is a painful new beginning: a new beginning for Trey, for me, for each member of our family, for each of his friends and all who ever knew him in any way. It is impossible to calculate how far reaching the effects of this event are or will become.

I am angry when I hear the words, "he passed." What does that mean? Does it mean he passed by me? Trey would never do that. Does it mean he passed in front of me or behind me or passed me on the street or passed Go and collected $200? What does that mean," passed?" Has he left us behind? Trey would never willingly leave us.

De-ceased: to depart from life. Trey did not depart from life. He continues to live in and through me. He lives in the life of his father, his sister, his wife, his children and countless others; family, friends and acquaintances. He has not deceased. He has not ceased to be. I chose to believe Trey's and every life brought forth here and now is endless. I don't believe this simply to find comfort. I believe this because this is what my life's experience has taught me to believe.

I am angered that we have not found better questions to ask of the grieving than, "How are you doing?" or "Are you o.k.?" There are no answers for these questions. Not after the loss of a loved one, any loved one, and particularly not after the greatest loss, a mother's loss of her child. It is a fierce grief that gradually becomes even fiercer because with support and guidance it becomes a grief that encompasses all grief and still is able to lift its head with hope. Parker Palmer says, "There are some human experiences that only the heart can comprehend and only heart-talk can convey." Then he continues, "—-heartbreak and depression, two of the most isolating and disabling things I know can evoke the heart's capacity to employ tension in the service of life."

Sometimes in my mind I am angry, hurt, fearful and resentful. At times I am exhausted, overwhelmed, heart-broken and confused. However, in my heart I have been given the capacity, as each of us has, to discover gratitude, joy, hope and love. At any given moment I am a paradox held together by mercy. If you ask how I am, I would say I am mourning the loss of my only son, my youngest child, Howard Volney Tygrett III, better know as Trey, born May 25, 1970, who died suddenly of a heart attack at age 40 in the early morning hours of December 25, 2010. At the same time, I would tell you I am surrounded and sustained by love. I am at-oneness. I have found truth in the words, "Blessed are those who mourn, for they shall be comforted." The truth of how I am is: in my mourning I am comforted.

TIMELESSNESS

Nothing ends.
I ponder this deep knowing
as I sit in the old wooden swing
my toes slightly pushing against
the rocky creek bank
creating constant motion:
back and forth, back and forth,
the chain creaks, u-huh, u-huh, u-huh.
Sunbeams play tag
across the clear water's surface.

I hear their voices from
another time in this time
that never ends,
"Drop now. Drop! Drop!"
He swings tightly grasping the old triangle,
his body propels forward until just above
the deep center of the swimming hole
he laughs then lets himself
swing back once more to catch
tree limbs along the bank.
Then pushing off again
he calls out "This time is it! Watch me!"
Youthful companions reply,
"You can do it! Let go!"
Splash! I watch him drop.
His lean, agile body submerges
for an instant
then quickly resurfaces.
He shakes the wetness from his curly locks,
arms extended in quick strokes,
legs kicking eagerly
he heads back to shore
ready for another try.

He is here and not here.
He has left and has remained.
I shed a tear, then smile
with deepest gratitude.

Judy Beene Myers

II

"During many nights in recent years and many mornings when I awake, I have felt like building an altar, for I did not believe that I could have felt this much pain and survived.

But I have. There is a resurrection."
—Janet Hoffman

"Life only demands from you the strength you possess.

Only one feat is possible—-not to have run away."
—Dag Hammarskjold

The days between January 2, when we returned to Austin from Brownsville, and January 22 when we sat in the International Bible Church in Clarkston, Georgia for a memorial service in the town Trey served as mayor, seemed to have been a period of my fading in and out of conscious awareness of life itself. The one thing I was able to do was not run away.

On waking each morning I lay in bed asking myself if this was really happening. My own grief was so all-encompassing that I had little or no energy for considering the grief of others, not even those closest to me. It seems, as I reflect back now, it was a selfish sort of grief. On one hand I wanted everyone around me to acknowledge my despair. At the same time I wanted to be left alone. I yearned for someone to restore my connection to my son, in some way to reclaim for me the life that was. It took and continues to take the healing of time to discover my closest connection to Trey is my life itself as it is now: life resting in the fullness of nature, life in a kayak softly gliding down a river, life in the chords of a guitar strumming and the tapping of twirling feet, life in spontaneous unexpected gestures of love. For many months after my son's death I could not feel life. All I could feel was the darkness of grief. I know not how I managed to get through that first month. It was a pure gift of grace. I was carried in a stream of love by the essence of love expressed in gestures of others and the sounds of silence.

On January 20 my husband, Ed, and I traveled to Atlanta. At the airport as we walked to baggage claim, I was aware this was the first time I had arrived there that Trey or Amy did not meet me at the curb. Tears flowed softly as we rode the Amtrak to pick up a rental car.

Where was he? Sometimes I felt I could jump off the train and run find him before he got away. I have had that feeling many times since. Now I catch him in unexpected dreams, I catch him in messages of him from some other place. I catch him in ways I have never caught him before. Our games of tag will never be the same.

It is surely no coincidence that at the same time I am writing this I am reading Parker Palmer's *Healing the Heart of Democracy*. In it he expresses the difference he understands between a heart being shattered and a heart being broken open: "If you hold your knowledge of self and the world wholeheartedly, your heart will at times get broken by loss, failure, betrayal or death. What happens next in you and the world around you depends on *how* your heart breaks. If it breaks *apart* into a thousand pieces, the result may be anger, depression and disengagement. If it breaks *open* into greater capacity to hold the complexities and contradictions of human experience, the result may be new life."

I understand these words to mean that a shattered heart, one broken into pieces, leaves one in a state of desolation and destruction with little or nothing significant left to offer the life force. While a heart broken open is able to release its grief and receive through mercy a grace sufficient to be able to open to new possibilities to extend into the world. Initially after learning of my son's death, I experienced a shattering of my heart. When I cried out with the hopelessness of despair, I was met by love that has and continues to break my heart open.

Sufi Master Hazrat Khan says, "God breaks our heart open again and again and again until it stays open."

I continue to experience periods of anguish that I understand as a feeling rather than despair which I believe is a state of being hopeless. When I allow grief to flow through me with all the energy it requires, my heart once again opens and I am able to embrace *the complexities and contradictions of my own experience* and discover *a newness of life.*

Deep within I have always known, with a knowing I am certain each of us possesses that my greatest yearning is to live this life I have been given in all its fullness. That is what my son would want for me: for me to live my most authentic life. I knew even in the face of this death that I had no choice but to turn toward each moment given me and that has made all the difference; that has brought forth my deepest grieving, and in so doing has turned me toward the vastness of my life as it is now.

On December 26 when Amy, her parents, my son's father and I went together to the funeral home in Harlingen, Texas, I was asked by the group to write Trey's obituary. My tribute to him included, "Trey loved life and his family and people in general, particularly the marginalized and disadvantaged. He loved to play the guitar and sing while his children danced. He loved to surprise his wife with something special when she least expected it. He loved kayaking, hiking and camping. He loved to stop and visit and lend a helping hand to anyone in need."

At the time of his death, Trey, Amy and their children were visiting her parents for a Christmas family reunion. Trey was then assistant manager of the REI store in Burford, Georgia, working at what he loved most: anything dealing with the outdoors. He was also serving as mayor of Clarkston, Georgia, having been elected in the fall of 2009 and sworn in January 2010, just a little over 11 months prior to his death.

Trey and Amy had purchased a home in the small Atlanta suburb just two years prior. Clarkston is situated just outside the perimeter of the I25 loop around Atlanta that separates the city from suburbia. The ethnically diverse town whose motto is, "small town, big heart" was originally a railroad town. Due to availability of affordable housing and close proximity to public transportation, Clarkston was designated a refugee resettlement community by the Office of Refugee Resettlement. Over 2500 refugees resettle annually in DeKalb County where Clarkston is located. A town of only 1.1 square miles is home to over 7500 residents representing more than 50 countries. Time Magazine has called Clarkston the most diverse square mile in America.

From his early childhood I remember Trey caring for those he considered to be treated unfairly, denied their rights, those less fortunate or suffering any kind of loss. I called him Captain Underdog, the main character in a cartoon he watched regularly as a child. He would mimic the character, saying, "Never fear, Underdog is here!" In a very short time as a Clarkston resident he saw and believed he could make a positive difference for the citizens there. He did.

On frequent visits there I discovered something of myself. Until living on a daily basis and experiencing a community that was 59% black, 17% Asian, 13% white and included many other ethnic groups I would not have admitted that, in fact, I was not as open-minded as I would like myself and others to believe. The neighborhood in which my very young grandchildren resided was in no way similar to the upper middle class and wealthy neighborhoods of North Dallas in which Trey's father and I had grown up and had raised our own children.

While spending time in such an environment, I was brought face to face with and had to acknowledge my own fear and often discomfort in associating with people who were markedly different from me. Prior to these experiences though I thought I was tolerant but I was tolerant only to a degree. I discovered there is a vast difference between brief encounters with those of different ethnic, cultural and religious backgrounds and living with diversity on a daily basis. I had to surrender my own stories of who I should associate with and who my children's and grandchildren's neighbors should be.

While in Clarkston I often cared for my grandchildren alone at home while Trey and Amy were at work. For the first time in my life I learned to honestly see people who were different from me. I frequently walked the children in their diverse neighborhood. We shopped at the huge DeKalb County International Market side by side with people from all over the globe. We attended the International Bible Church, home to members from more than 15 countries. The church also houses congregations of Ethiopians, Sudanese, Liberians and French West Africans. We often watched the Fugees, the nationally recognized refugee soccer team, practice at a nearby park.

These were the people that mourned the loss of and honored my son with a Celebration of Life with his family, classmates from The Webb School in Bell Buckle, Tennessee and Lambuth University in Jackson, Tennessee, national, state and local officials and childhood friends. In my own tribute there I said, "Trey's family is overwhelmed with the love for him expressed to us in so many ways and by so many, often including comments such as, "It was never about Trey.

It was always about others—-I have never heard Trey say anything bad about anyone—-Trey never had one group of friends, he liked everyone for who he or she was."

It was here in Clarkston, the town my son brought me to experience, that I learned greater open mindedness and open heartedness. In Clarkston my son taught me a deeper concern for others. "Just be nice, Mom," he would say, "That's all any of us need to do, just be nice." My stories of myself changed as I was no longer the same after learning to listened to the stories of these others. I understood as I experienced diversity in this small Georgia town the truth of the words of possibility: "Let there be peace on earth, and let it begin with me."

I AM YOU, YOU ARE ME

You have gone.

I cannot clasp your hand

or reach across the table

to pass the bread basket.

I search finding you

only when I close my eyes.

I see you

in not seeing you.

Still, dreaming of you,

my heart sings out

with joyful songs.

You have not gone.

your soul

has blended

into mine.

—-Judy Beene Myers

III

"As long as we see what has come to pass as being unfair, we'll be a prisoner of what might have been—-

I offer what has surprised me in my pain: that life is not fair, but unending in it's capacity to change us; that compassion is fair and feeling is just; and that we are not responsible for all that befalls us, only for how we receive it and how we hold each other up along the way."
—Mark Nepo, The Book of Awakening

"I don't know how to do this." I remember saying those words over and over through my sobs in the early morning hours when I learned of Trey's death.

"Miss Eissie will help me. I know she will." Miss Eissie was my grandmother to whom I was very close as a child and young adult. Her only son, the middle of her three children, was killed in a car accident when he was 27 years old. He left a wife and one son not yet a year old.

My grandmother lived 88 years. She lived a full, meaningful life. Her presence here was a gift to five generations of her family and to a large community of friends. She lived on over 30 years after her child's death. I knew that she must know, even if she was no longer here in body, how to do this: how to live with and through this grief and to become able to emerge out into the light once more. I knew then, as I know now, the essence of my grandmother guides me. All mothers, known and unknown to me, who have ever lost children are my guides, my teachers, my support, my strength, my hope.

Even now I do not know how to do this. I am learning with each new day. As I look back since the time of Trey's death, I see I have changed. I realize now that during the first few months following the loss of my son I just did the best I could, often not fully aware of what I was doing. It was difficult to be in what once seemed familiar places with familiar people in familiar circumstances. Nothing seemed familiar any more. I felt hurled into an entirely different world. I seemed to be functioning from an unfamiliar state of mind.

I recognized almost nothing of myself and very little of my family and friends. Once, I tried explaining myself to another mother who had lost her child, saying I felt fearful and anxious most of the time. She said to me, "I believe it can best be described as feeling like a burn victim. You think that if someone touches you, you will flinch from the raw pain, your skin will fall off and you will break apart." She gave words to my confusion.

Sometime after the fist six months my daughter said to me one day, "Mom, you are not the only one who is grieving. How do you think it feels for me to have lost my brother, my only sibling, the one I thought would be with me when you and dad are sick or when you die?"

She did not speak those words gently. She spoke them factually and pointedly. Because I heard what she said, I was able to begin my turn toward extending compassion: compassion to myself, my family, my extended family, my friends, Trey's friends, the unlimited community of suffering of which I am a part.

A few years ago, after my mother died, one of my teachers said to me, "It's time for you to take your place." I did not agree. I was not ready at that time to let go of all that must be let go of to become an elder. I have never easily or readily relinquished anything in my life. I have had to learn the hard way. I have had to have it done unto me. Now, faced with this tragic event in my life and hearing my daughter's words, I became aware that, in fact, this death was not just about its affect on me. Now, faced with this tragic event in my life and hearing my daughter's words, I became aware, that in fact, this death was not just about its effect on me. I suddenly realized I had become their elder. There were children, grandchildren, family and friends who needed me. My focus had to be on more than just my own needs. I had to begin to consider what I had to offer others. So as best I could I began imagining what it might be like to walk in the shoes of others affected by this death. Gradually, I became more willing to experience the pain of so many I knew were suffering: those I knew directly and those I was brought into contact with indirectly by the daily barrage of tragic news. I began to understand for the first time through my family and friends and then extending out into my community and into the world how deeply we all need each other, how truly we all are connected.

I continue to learn moment to moment "how to do this." One morning I went for a regular appointment with my young female dermatologist. She recently gave birth to a baby daughter. We talked about children, "How many children do you have?" she asked. I hate this question but I love the questioner. I said, "My son died. Remember I told you last time I was here. I also have a daughter. I have two children."

"I am so sorry," she said, "I forgot."

"Please don't worry about it. Today is a good day. Some days are better than others."

"How are you doing?"

There was the question again. The one I cannot answer except to say,

"I am doing o.k. I am recovering," while wondering what is really happening here.

Later, walking to the grocery store, I crossed a busy intersection. Approaching me from the opposite direction, a carelessly dressed, out of shape middle aged man, walked past mumbling something I could only detect as,

20

"I love you!"

It's best if I don't think about these things. It's best if I just accept the astonishment of the moment with humility and gratitude. I smiled and kept on going. That is all I really know to do.

IV

RED SHIRT

Has anyone seen the boy who used to come here?

Round-faced troublemaker, quick to find a joke, slow

to be serious. Red shirt,

perfect coordination, sly,

strong muscles, with things always in his pocket: red flute,

ivory pick, polished and ready for his talent.

You know that one.

Have you heard stories about him?

Pharaoh and the whole Egyptian world

collapsed for such a Joseph.

I'd gladly spend years getting word

of him, even third or fourth-hand.
—-Rumi

    I don't know if it is because I am growing older or if it is that grief has taught me to experience life in a new way, but often now as I sit silently on our patio gazing out on the trees and up into the sky, my memories seem to be of the present moment rather than occurrences from the past. I feel I know, in fact, that nothing ever ends. This is more than just a remembering. I have discovered a sense of being with a specific incident, place, person from what we call the "past" in a way that was and is and evermore shall be.

I am not surprised when silently I see them still playing in the creek-bed: three young boys splashing, running up and down the flow of the stream. They stop, peer down into the shallow depths of bright, clear water attempting to catch a frog or minnow, then settle for collecting rocks. Occasionally they uncover a fossil. One stuffs it into his pocket to examine more closely on another day.

Now is the time for rapid moving on. One boy follows another. The curly, auburn haired boy is usually in the lead. "Wait for me, Trey," the others call but he slows only slightly. They know they must be quick to keep his pace.

Later they begin the thoughtful activity of gathering larger stones, lining them uniformly across the creek bed creating a make-shift dam interspersed with miniature waterfalls. One picks up a dried brown cottonwood leaf and hurries upstream to carefully place it in the water's flow. They watch and wait, curiously laughing. Will their dam restrain the sailing leaf-boat or will its' uncharted gliding lead it into the tiny whirlpool and carry it over the waterfall into the mighty creek to float downstream forever?

I see them now as I saw them then: Trey, Ned and Peter his pals from next door, parading usually in that order.

Could I call this, one of uncountable memories, just that: a memory, or are these moments so real and present even now that they are in fact ongoing? Do I even need to know the answer to this question? Perhaps all I need to know is simply this: there is a comfort that arises out of grief. I am comforted when I allow my riven heart to offer its split openness as a vessel to receive ever-present love and unexpected joy.

There is no relationship more filled with continual grasping and letting go than that between a mother and her child. No other relationship requires such total surrender as a mother when she sends "flesh of my flesh" out into the vastness of the world and then hopefully, anxiously awaits homecoming.

We bear them forth with glorious pain into life here and now. We courageously launch them into the uncertainty of their own futures. We do not bear them for death. When that unthinkable event happens, we take them back again. We hold them again in our bodies and souls, finally to birth them once more in a new way, into a new life. Having given ourselves to motherhood we have no other choice.

More than a year after Trey's death, a good friend sought my counsel concerning a matter I can best describe as allowing her young adult daughter to make her own mistakes.

I replied with the following email:

There is nothing harder than letting go of our children. No one knows that better than another mother. I have found comfort in the image of Mary, the mother of Jesus, and her words, "Let it be done to me as You will." Mary gave voice to total surrender and that is what is asked of all mothers.

Our children are not ours to keep. We have them for a while, then release them with hope they will become who they were designed to be in whatever way that happens which is each of their paths, not ours. We help them learn to fly. It is up to us to let them try their wings.

Then we return to the nest feeling at first lonely and afraid; fearful not only for our child but afraid that we will no longer recognize who we are. So we sit in the nest silently and wait patiently until the seed of a new birth begins to grow. We begin to follow the path that is uniquely our own. It is more than just birthing human lives, it is birthing whatever we feel called to co-create here and now.

24

Birthing our children is preparation for even greater birthing that is beyond our imagining. We must be present to that silent beat constantly pulsing in our hearts. It will show us the way It is the beat of our ancestors' hearts and our children's hearts entwined within our own. Julian of Norwich, one of the best known Christian mystics from 14th century England portrayed Christ as the nurturing mother. She believed all of humanity has life through the love of a mother. She is often quoted as saying, "All shall be well. All manner of all things shall be well." I have come to believe in my mother's heart the truth of this deep mystery.

I wish I were able to consistently act from this truth. I do not. Now, as I write in my second year since Trey died, I find grief slams me like an unexpected tidal wave, powerful and consuming. A dear friend who lost her husband and young child in an automobile accident many years ago explained to me that following the first year after the loss of a beloved, one is no longer insulated by shock. Only the bare and brutal facts of what has occurred remain.

As I move into acceptance I find I am sometimes angry, even angry at Trey for dying. I am aware of my reluctance to move out into unfamiliar places with unfamiliar people. I am taking baby steps into uncharted territory. Some days I feel stronger. Other days I wish I were a turtle and could retreat into the dark, comforting silence of my shell. I do know I am moving more and more into living with and in the new reality of my life. I am beginning to allow my son's life to emerge through me in a new and different way. I am confident in my knowing that if I keep as my intent to remain open and available I will be shown the way.

During the first year following Trey's death, early on many mornings I drove past a particular intersection at approximately the same time each day. It was the beginning of a new school semester. Daily, I noticed a young boy with a bike and his mother standing close beside him. I observed as the light changed from red to green the mother nodded to her child and together they walked the bike across the intersection. After a few days of watching this ritual, I witnessed a change. One morning the child was at the intersection alone, poised and ready to take off as soon as the light signaled go. Looking more closely I saw, waiting a few feet behind him, his mother silently but totally attending to her child and his surroundings. This image will forever remain in my consciousness.

LETTING GO

Like a bird learning to fly

the young boy stands on one leg

his bike leaning inward toward his body,

opposite leg bent, foot poised on petal,

ready for take off

the instant the light turns green.

In the background standing stately

as a lighthouse

his mother attentively watches

beaming her guiding light,

prayerfully holding him

in her heart,

his image mirrored

in her eyes.

Stilling anxiousness

with soft, deep breaths

her mothers' dream unfolds

launching her child

into the world,

with hope to bring him

safely home again.

—-Judy Beene Myers

V

Photographs. There are photographs of family in every room in our home. Photographs in silver frames, home-made frames from grandchildren, wooden frames announcing, "Look at us now!" "You're the best," "Celebrate Love." There are boxes of photographs on closet shelves and a basket of snapshots sits on a bench in the entryway. One morning some months after Trey's death I felt an urgency to know I had every photograph of him placed carefully in one location. This is a continuing project: one that I return to as I feel able.

Trey's last day on earth is captured in pictures he took of the children playing on the beach. I smile when I look at them. There are many pictures taken that evening of Amy's family's Christmas Eve celebration. I was unable to look at them for many months. When finally I went through them, I was pleased to see how well and happy Trey appeared. Rarely am I able to pause and gaze at a single photograph. Perhaps as time passes I will become ready to fully attend to each one. I have discovered the most comfort in looking through photos of my son's childhood.

My mother once said to me, "You will always remember the look and feel of your children's bodies. No matter how old you become, when you think of your children, you will remember the outlines of their naked forms, how it felt to touch them, the form of each small muscle, the lines in each small hand. You will never forget these things." I know what she meant. The body of her child is imprinted on a mother's soul, embodied in her senses. I am reminded through photographs that Trey's life is so embedded in mine that there can be no separation.

I often receive new pictures of his children, my grand-children. I see their resemblances to their father. I discover him anew in them. When we introduce Alice Elizabeth and Ty to some new experience, I often hear my daughter, Carroll, say, "Mom, wouldn't Trey love this!"

When we are all together out under the night sky, I hear his children exclaim to the moon, "Daddy in the moon, here we are." They tell me he is there watching them all the time. I agree. We sing together, "I see the moon, the moon sees me." I have learned to respond with childlike caring to my grandchildren when they express their grief in the manner of a three and four-year-old. I listen and wait for openings and opportunities to gradually reveal their father to them as only I will be able to do.

Trey loved to kayak, hike and play his guitar. I sense my son intimately when I am outdoors experiencing nature. This past spring I adopted a garden at Mayfield Park, an historic estate give to the City of Austin as a public park. Mayfield is like a cocoon holding me in my transformation. During the ten years we have lived here the park's ponds, trails, plants, trees and creek have offered a special place of solace for me. I have spent many hours there in silent reflection, walking, just being and be-coming.

Much of my grieving has been done at Mayfield Park and so it seemed a natural place to adopt a family garden to honor Trey. I found a perfect site where a cedar and a palm tree grow side by side. The sight and smells of cedars have been familiar to me throughout my life. The palm trees were brought to Austin from the Texas coastal area where Amy and the children now live.

I am not an accomplished gardener. I am learning on the job. Texas soil is hard and dry. Turning dirt and planting require time and patience. When I work in the garden, I have no fixed deadline. I allow the tasks at hand to overtake me. I become the tasks.

I met with a volunteer coordinator and was told my primary job would be to clear away the invasive vine, Cat's Claw: an unending effort. If left unchecked, the vine rapidly overtakes the garden becoming large enough to wrap around trees and choke them. I use a trowel to dig down into the soil loosening and extracting the nutlike seed from which the roots emerge. Removing Cat's Claw has become a ritualistic metaphoric means of working with my sorrow. The vine represents my deep grief which also springs forth from a primary source and reaches out with catlike claws grasping, attempting to choke my life source. As I work slowly to eliminate each new sprout, I am relieved. I feel a release of pain and an allowing for an opening for something new to emerge in its place. Being with and experiencing the earth and the process of birth and death eternally surrounding and contained within its sphere gently leads me back into my present moment.

Recently at Mayfield I witnessed a mother peacock and five chicks in an adjoining garden. Gradually they wandered into our garden, then out into an open area of the park. The mother bird constantly held her head erect, her eyes alert and focused straight ahead. She moved slowly forward with a back and forth swaying movement of her neck, her body always slightly ahead of her chicks. Occasionally she glanced to one side and then the other. She never lowered her gaze. She remained vigilantly aware of any approaching danger. Her body displayed the fierceness of her loving concern for her children.

I have witnessed this fierceness before. I have seen it on film in an incident when a mother elephant successfully defended her calf against the onslaught of a pack of hyenas. The mother elephant displayed a "determined furiousness," which is how Webster defines the word fierceness. On another occasion, I watched a television news account of a mother lying on top of her two daughters during a violent tornado, saving her children's lives and in the process losing both her legs. I witnessed this fierceness in the face of my daughter-in-law photographed Christmas morning as she courageously joined her children in unwrapping their gifts all the while knowing her husband, their, father, had died just a few short hours before.

My understanding of the word fierceness in relation to caring is the willingness to risk everything for the life of another or others. What exemplifies that fierceness or offers that understanding of the word to the world more perfectly than the love of a mother for her child?

I am reminded of the words of Zen Buddhism's Metta Sutra:

"Even as the mother at the risk of her life watches over and protects her only child,

So with a boundless mind should one cherish all living things.

Suffusing love over the entire world,

Above, below, and all around, without limit.

So let one cultivate an infinite good will toward the whole world,

Standing or walking, sitting or lying down,

During all one's waking hours,

Let one practice the way with gratitude.

Not holding to fixed views,

Endowed with insight, freed from sense appetites,

One who achieves the way

Will be freed from the duality of birth and death."

Most mornings before dawn, I walk outside just to feel the morning air. It never fails to greet me with promise. I am reminded I am still breathing in and out, here and now for some unknowable reason. I am now more comfortable with the mystery of it all. I have discovered that when everything else is taken away, there is nothing left but gratitude, there is nothing left to offer but everything, there is nothing left to express but kindness. In reaching out to my natural surroundings to rediscover my son I always find something more. I am always changed.

BEARERS OF LIGHT

The darkness of night begins to fade,

light returns: visibility.

All creation begins to stir.

Birds recognize that they are light.

Each feathered creature begins to sing

its welcoming song.

Each sounds its own unique melody.

Barking dogs remember who they are,

as do bees and crickets in the fields.

Wildflowers stretch and open

in praise of sunbeams

and also the grasses and trees.

Brooks bubble forth.

Turtles crawl out from hiding

to perch on rocks, bask in warmth.

Sleeping humans begin stirring

Responding to a signal from within that says,

"Now is the time to begin again."

So each one does:

one faltering, another eagerly,

each of them together

with all that awakens

are bearers of the light.
—-Judy Beene Myers

VI

"energy of some kind is a fundamental prerequisite for being—

Some quotes from individuals reflect this—

'When I am truly centered, I am a wave on an infinite ocean, a part of something immeasurably deep, endlessly vast, totally without boundaries. Beneath—-and in—-that little wave which is my body and my "me" lies all the re-source and potential of creation.'"
—Gerald G. May, Will and Spirit

"When your time comes, may you have

every blessing and strength you need.

May there be a beautiful welcome for you

In the home your are going to.

You are not going somewhere strange,

Merely back to the home you have never left."
—John O'Donohue, from Entering Death

There is a Presence. It is with and in the Presence that my son, Trey, abides. I am certain of this. I have experienced this Presence.

34

I awakened around 2 a.m. one morning in January 2010, shortly after returning home from Trey's swearing in as Mayor of Clarkston. I went into the bathroom. A few minutes later as I returned to the bedroom, I collapsed to the floor. Every muscle and bone in my body seemed to have dissolved. I told myself I must get to Ed. I knew he would be unable to hear me.

My husband wears a hearing aid which he removes at night. He cannot hear anything without it. Some unexplainable power enabled me to raise up, crawl to the side of the bed, pull up, click on the lamp, and reach out to arouse Ed before collapsing once again.

In the immediate confusion of Ed calling 911 and the dog frantically barking I attempted to crawl down the hallway. I managed to stand momentarily. Collapsing a third time I totally let go. I surrendered to what was happening.

Later my granddaughter asked,

"Did you see the light?"

"Yes and no," I answered.

I explained I did not see anything. It was an experience. In those moments lying on the floor I was held in the embrace of overwhelming peace and comfort with the assurance that everything would be alright. I believe it was love.

Something told me, "You are not going anywhere. Nothing is required of you. You are going to lay here. You will be taken care of."

When we lived on the Outer Banks of North Carolina, a favorite thing of mine to do was take a ferry from Cedar Point to Okracoke Island. It was about a two hour trip. I would often walk to the back of the ferry and look out at the horizon, my chin resting on the boat's railing. As I gazed at the point where ocean meets sky, I was always fascinated by a space seemingly created between the two elements by the listing of the ferry. The up and down motion of the boat appeared to open a space in which a ribbon of light emerged as if it always exists there between sky and sea. I felt a sense of belonging witnessing this mystery, a sense of embrace. That feeling of belonging returned as I lay on the floor near death.

Thomas Merton says:

"God is near to us at the point that is just before final destruction

Take away everything else down to that point of final destruction

and the last little bit that's left before destruction, a little kernel

of gold which is the essence of you—-and there is God protecting

It—-and this is something terrific.—-"

He continues:

"The freedom that matters is the capacity to be in contact with that center. Because it is from that center that everything comes—-
But we don't normally get into that center unless we're brought to the edge of what looks like destruction. In other words, we have to be facing the possibility of the destruction of everything else to know this will not be destroyed."

Merton says when one dies, that little kernel of gold is all that is left. That is one's essence and the essence of all that exists.

One of my teachers told me of an old Zen poem. It was about a warrior who sharpened his sword daily until at least it was razor sharp. One day he was confronted by death. He pulled the sword out of its sheath and it broke in two. He had nothing left to fight with. It was then he realized there was nothing left to fight.

I recall feeling cool night air enter the house when my husband opened our front door to await the ambulance. I silently welcomed its refreshing touch. Lying on the floor near death I knew I had nothing left to fight. I surrendered. All I remember of the EMS team that came to give assistance was their voices. Later I learned that hearing is the last sense of awareness one loses before death. A few minutes later as I was carried out on a stretcher a soft winter mist fell on my face. I felt it as a sort of baptism.

When I was admitted to Seton Hospital's ICU, Ed was told my veins had collapsed and I had only a 15 to 30 minute window for survival. Time, they hoped, that would allow the nurses to be able to find a vein strong enough to administer an IV and begin blood transfusions. Ultimately I received six pints of blood. The following day I would be told by a nurse, "You are one for the records!"

I am here now because of Mercy and Grace which I believe are gifts of this loving Presence. It is the same loving Presence in which and with which I believe my son abides.

There are days I want to ask, "Did God get confused and take the wrong one of us?" However, I don't allow myself those questions as I know there are no answers. I do know there is a loving force holding each of us. I do know I am here because of the love, support and efforts of others, many of whom I will never know; strangers who gave their blood for me that I might live. I do know this abiding love eternally connects all of creation. I do know that death as we think of it in our western society is not an ending but a mysteriously beautiful new beginning.

As a result of this experience and prior to Trey's death I wrote a letter to my grandchildren in which I said:

" I recently confronted the fragility of my own life as I collapsed unexpectedly one night with a bleeding ulcer. When I was admitted to the hospital, I had barely enough blood remaining in my body to keep me alive until I was given a blood transfusion, received treatment and was gradually restored to health. I now understand the necessity of writing to you without delay of anything I feel important to share that might in some way be helpful along the way as each of you grows and matures.

We are all dying. From the moment we leave our mother's womb and enter the physical world, we begin to die. We live and we die at the same time. Isn't that amazing? From the very beginning of your lives, from the very first day you were each born you each began to die. At the same time you are continually being born into new, ever- expanding life.

When you emerge into the world, you die to being fed from a tube in your mother's womb, you die to living in a dark, cozy, comforting space within your mother's body. Dying is letting go. Dying is allowing something new to emerge.

The caterpillar dies to become the butterfly, the egg dies to become the chick, the blossom dies to become the seed to again become the new blossom, the tadpole becomes the frog, the child become the adolescent, then the adult, the mother becomes the grandmother. Everything is always be-coming or coming into being. It is the cycle of life.

I wish I could tell you that all you will each experience will be happiness and everything will always be just the way you wish it, but in reality I must tell you that life as it is often seems unfair. It is not what happens to us that is so important. It is how we view our circumstances and how we face each moment that matters. It is about relationship beginning with your relationship to yourselves and extending to your relationships with your families, your friends, your communities and your world."

As I reread my own words I remember the words of my teacher: "Now you must be Trey's eyes and ears and hands. You are Trey's voice in the world. You are Trey's heart."

So often I have not wanted to be those things. I have wanted to once again be the mother of the son who lives in the world along side her, but I am not. Now I am learning, reluctantly at first but gradually more willingly, to become the words of my teacher. There are painful moments but I am also discovering joy.

Reflecting on my near death experience I also wrote: "Now I see that death has always been a major part of my life. I understand that life and death continually relinquish and welcome each other. I am learning to accept the beauty of the coexistence of the two and the fundamental principle that there can be no life without death. Life and death will forever walk side by side."

In Mary Oliver's poem to her dog, Percy, following his death, I find words expressing this eternal coexistence of life and death and once again I am comforted.

"The first time Percy came back

he was not sailing on a cloud.

He was loping along the sand as though he had come a great way.

"Percy," I cried out, and reached to him—-

those white curls—-

but he was unreachable. As music

is present yet you can't touch it.

"Yes, it's all different," he said.

"You're going to be very surprised."

But I wasn't thinking of that. I only

wanted to hold him. "Listen," he said,

"I miss that too.

And now you'll be telling stories

of my coming back

and they won't be false, and they won't be true,

but they'll be real."

And then, as he used to, he said, "Let's go!"

and we walked down the beach together.
—Mary Oliver

VII

Smoke Signals
—a dedication—

There are people on a parallel way. We do not

see them often, or even think of them often,

but it is precious to us that they are sharing

the world. Something about how they have accepted

their lives, or how the sunlight happens to them

helps us to hold the strange, enigmatic days

in line for our own living. It is important

that these people know this recognition, but

it is also important that no purpose or obligation

related to this be intruded into their lives.

This book intends to be for anyone, but especially

for those on that parallel way: here is a smoke

signal, unmistakable but unobtrusive—-we are

following what comes, going through the world,

knowing each others, building our little fires.
—William Stafford

Near the first anniversary of my son's death I received this poem in an email from my dear friend Jolynn. It has happened throughout my life that the right people have appeared to share my journey just when I have needed them. At first meeting I did not initially realize the impact he or she would have on me as I traveled my path. I have, however, felt on our first encounters the magnetic pull of hearts being brought together as one.

The day after the memorial service for Trey in Georgia, Ed and I returned to Austin. The following morning I left for a five-day contemplative retreat in Taos, New Mexico. I would be in close community with fellow pilgrims, each on their own inward journey, many of whom I had been on retreats with previously and others who were new to me.

I barely knew what I was doing from moment to moment. One of my teachers, also a leader of the retreat said to me, "You need to do this."

He did not say, "I think this would be good for you," or "We really want you there." He simply said quietly, "You need to do this."

Often I recall a story told to me by the late Fr. Pat Hawk on the day his teacher, Robert Aiken, founder of the Diamond Sangha in Honolulu, died. I sat in a circle with Fr. Pat while on retreat on the Senora Desert. He read from Aiken's book, *Zen Master Raven,* concerning Raven's departure from the Tall Spruce Community. In that account when it became time for Raven to leave, a hush came over the community,

"Its time to be moving on," Raven said.

Grouse could be heard sniffling. At last Porcupine asked, "Do you have any last words for us?" Raven said, "Trust."

A month after Trey's death and two days after his memorial service, I felt so much grief and brokenness. I was in such pain that I needed to be told what to do. I was certain, though, even in the state I was in, that I could trust my teachers. I could trust Jolynn to lead me there. I could trust the group I would be on retreat with. I was completely dependent on the generosity of others.

Most of the first year following my son's death I was incapable of doing more than was absolutely necessary. I was unable to make arrangements for the trip to Taos. Jolynn did that for me.

Grief teaches us to ask and to gratefully receive. Grief teaches us to let go. Grief teaches us it is o.k. to rest dependently in the arms of others. I allowed another's caring attention and actions to get me on the plane, arrange for a rental car and drive us to the lodge where the retreat was to be held.

I remember the journey up the road winding along the Rio Grande River, through the valleys, the hills enfolding us from every direction, the sounds of the flowing river and winter breezes sighing softly through the evergreens. There was very little conversation. There was simply communion in the unspoken giving and receiving of blessings. In looking back at my time in Taos, I cannot remember the theme of the retreat, the materials we used, the discussions, the content or any of the usual things I take home from such an event to ponder, reflect on and journal about.

One sunny afternoon I walked to the square and into a shop or two. I always enjoy looking at Native American art: the pottery, jewelry and crafts. I returned to the lodge by walking through the park. I found a secluded bench and sat down alone. I broke into uncontrollable sobs.

Later I would learn I was experiencing guilt as begins to happen to one when discovering unexpected moments of joy in the face of grief. I needed the guidance of those who work with trauma and loss to speak for me the right words to express feelings that seemed overwhelming and foreign.

The ever-present darkness of those early months of loss held all the things I wished never to feel so often and with such intensity: anger, frustration, resentment, doubt, betrayal, uncertainty, regret, all of which could be traced back to the constant fear of unending loss and the inability to ever live life fully again.

I hated my life. I remember at that time and for many months following, saying, "I hate this. I am exhausted. This will never end. I will never regain any kind of balance. I don't want to do this any more. I can't do this."

But there were hearts and arms and ears and eyes and hands reaching out to me, holding me and I, in my innermost being, somehow allowed the decision to be made to focus on the love that surrounded me knowing it would, in the end, sustain and nurture me back to life.

Those days at Taos were the beginning of my allowing others to enter in and participate in my grief. I remember Sarah's gentle voice and tender touches. I remember Charley sitting next to me. Throughout the week the two of us built an altar to Trey. I contributed words and objects of remembrance. Charley discovered natural materials in the surrounding landscape and created a tribute to my son, which he unveiled as our small group sat together in the final circle before departure.

Trey's favorite song, "Blackbird," played softly in the background.

"Blackbird singing in the dead of

Take these broken wings and let them fly

All your life you were only waiting

For this moment to arise."
—-Paul McCartney

On the cool winter afternoons in Taos, Peg, a Buddhist teacher for many of us and at the time a retreat participant, led our group in meditation walks. As the fading sun reflected off the shadowy face of Taos Mountain we reverently walked single file down the snowy slope to the labyrinth. Our footsteps slowly traced its pattern. We each paused to be held in its center before returning to the path leading outward back into the world.

Later I asked Peg, "Did you bring a copy of the Bodhisattva Vow with you?" She told me she had not.

The Mahayana Buddhist Vow states one's intent is to, above all else, help end the suffering of all sentient beings. I had left behind a copy of it lying on my desk at home.

When I saw Peg again, she handed me a page on which she had diligently and precisely hand printed the 38-line vow. I took it to my room and placed it carefully on the bedside table, a visual reminder that one's intent is something no circumstances can ever take away. One's intent can only be willingly relinquished. It is always a choice.

One evening I skipped dinner. Instead I went to my room, lay on the bed and cried. For a period of time that seemed forever, my sorrow was so deep I thought the tears would never cease.

After a while, Jolynn knocked on the door and came in to sit with me. I was relieved to have someone to pour my anger onto.

"See," I said, "I knew if you brought me here, this would happen. I should have never come. I am a complete mess!"

She sat there with that half smile on her face. I have grown use to it now. It is not a smile or a frown or a blank look. It is just her, "It will get better, honey," assuring expression.

"Maybe you should go have something to eat," she said finally.

"Only if no one looks at me or talks to me and if I don't have to sit by anyone," I replied.

"I can take care of that," came her usual welcomed reply in the face of my uncertainty. Again I allowed someone to lead me. Again I was fed. It was the bread of Christ broken for me in the presence of love. I felt a strength return, a peacefulness. Again I was comforted.

Each morning at daybreak I headed alone to the grounds of the art gallery just across the road from the lodge. There I walked a trail around a pond rimmed with ice, mirroring morning. Wildlife was awakening. Now and then I saw a redbird in the midst of the mild winter. I noticed budding signs of spring appearing on bare tree limbs. Tiny sparks of renewal began faintly awakening within the darkness of my soul.

I ended each day in Taos by turning out my lights, standing at the window and gazing up into the velvety dark night sky. It was the time of the full moon. Its light danced reflectively across the snow-patched pasture behind my room. I recognized familiar constellations as I scanned the night sky. Then my vision would become fixed in amazement on the Milky Way. I felt at once so small and alone and at the same time held in such vast wonder. Those nights under the stars I slept better than I had since Christmas Eve. I rested in a sound, unbroken sleep.

Embodying the miracles of creation in the darkness and light surrounded by the Sangre de Cristo Mountains, I began to faintly feel the light of wholeness return. I would call it seeds of resurrection. Fr. Richard Rohr says we have to begin with the first Bible, which is creation itself—-that God has revealed who God *is* through what *is*.

On those mornings and evenings in Taos held by creation itself revealed in the natural world and expressed through the goodness of those around me I experienced who God *is*. I was caught once more in that pulse of truth, that quiet everpresent strength that, no matter what is happening around us, forever sends us forth into our lives with hope.

I find moments of the awareness of the unquestion-able and ever-present connection of all living things come and go like the ebb and flow of the ocean. I live now with the constant assurance that silence will forever guide me home.

First poem since Trey entered the mystery—-

THE HIGH PLAINS AT 10 A.M.

Standing alone on the high plains
witnessing earth meeting sky
in every direction,
I sense I am surrounded by The Presence,
also infused by It
and totally supported.

Or is this just awareness
in the silence of the morning
of all this aliveness, this is-ness
available every moment
of my be-coming.

Held in a womb of wonder
my poet's soul awakes.
In awe I discover
this grief
in truth is love—-
immeasurable,
unspeakable,
unfathomable
love.

For Trey
Judy Beene Myers
February, 2011

VIII

"The Pilgrim look directly into the face of impermanence and finds there the solace that others find in the notion of heaven and eternal life. What is that source? Ha-ha! How truly beautiful everything is!"
—Robert Aiken, Original Dwelling Place

"Blessed are the peacemakers for they shall be called the children of God." Matt. 5:9

On the morning of Sept.11, 2001 I was in the kitchen preparing for the day. We lived in Jackson, Tennessee, where Trey worked with us managing J.B. Myers and Company, an outdoor retail business Ed and I owned at the time. Turning on the kitchen TV and glancing at the news, I was immediately startled by the scene appearing live from New York City. I watched as billowing smoke poured forth from one of the Twin Towers. Almost immediately, Trey called.

"Mom, do you have the news on? What do you think is happening."

I had learned through the years that when any out of ordinary event occurred to expect my children to call asking me as young adults just as they had as children to explain things, to give some sense or reason to what was happening.

"I don't know," I said, my eyes focused on the scene before me.

"Maybe there is just a fire—-a fire they will be able to get under control quickly."

That was not the case. We all know what unfolded that morning. The entire nation and world watched in total shock at the unexpected and tragic events of that day. Our country and the complete global society was thrown into collective trauma, the same type of trauma I experienced when learning of Trey's sudden death.

September 11, 2011 marked the 10th anniversary of events that changed, for most of us, the way we view ourselves, our nation and our world. In our humanness we will never again be the same. Our world will never be the same. The event of my son's death on December 25, 2010 changed forever the way I view myself, my relationships and each moment of my existence. My personal world will never again be the same as before that date. I am forever changed.

On the 10th Anniversary of 9/11 I spent much of the day watching the commemorative events on TV. It was nearly nine months after Trey's death and I was aware that I was more than just a spectator. I was drawn attentively to the coverage of events. As never before, I felt deeply involved in these tributes. As others bore witness to my pain over the unexpected death of my son, I now was bearing witness to the pain of individuals who had lost loved ones, the pain of a nation, the pain of the planet.

As I watched from my bedroom in deeply felt sorrow, I sensed something emerge as the entourage of dignitaries processed forward to take their places on the stage at the memorial for the victims of Flight 93. Leaders of both parties stood at allegiance, then seated themselves to face the audience. I do not recall all that as said honoring the courageous acts of those few. I do remember the poem, Souvenir of the Ancient World, by Carlos Drummond de Andrade, read by the nation's Poet Laureate, Robert Pinsky.

"Clara strolled in the garden with the children.

The water was golden under the bridges,

Other elements were blue and rose and orange,

A policeman smiled, bicycles passed,

A girl stepped onto the lawn to catch a bird,

The whole world, Germany, China,

All was quiet around Clara.

The Children looked at the sky: it was not forbidden.

Mouth, nose, eyes were open. There was no danger.

What Clara feared were the flu, the heat, the insects,

Clara feared missing the eleven o'clock trolley:

She waited for letters slow to arrive,

She couldn't always wear a new dress.

But she strolled in the garden,

In the morning!

They had gardens,they had mornings in those days!"

The words of the poem seem to call forth the place within the place where we each at our deepest level always truly reside. It is the place in which, from which humanity will always remain connected with every living cell of every living thing.

Following tributes and readings, those leading the ceremony rose and walked to the unveiling of the national memorial honoring the 40 men and women and one unborn child who died in the crash. As I watched each individual in the group, I was aware of the many deep disagreements among them, of times of disharmony. I recognized how my own opinions and critical views contributed to any lack of unity.

However, in those moments something else occurred. I experienced an emergence occurring from thousands of miles away. I felt life embracing itself, holding every living thing. Silently I felt a oneness with the beauty of the human spirit that, above everything else, emerged to capture the moment. All that was present in that present was The Presence Itself, Love.

Finally, it is this that will endure. It is this we will return to. When all our likes and dislikes are put aside, when all our preferences and judgments are forgotten, we will, like these men and women, at this moment, allow our spirits to flow into and become one with each other. Then we will send that message out into the universe. Then we will truly honor The Ancient World with and in peace.

During my grief process I have corresponded with Peter Herschock at the East-West Center in Honolulu. Gratefully during these months I have participated in studies of his profound works on Chan Buddhism. I have explained to him my current situation and expressed my gratitude for the way in which his work has helped me turn toward my own tragedy.

In a reply he said:

"Grief is not a 'universal' that can be gotten around without missing what it means and for what it might become as a means—-a way. Each of us, each time we experience grief, only moves forward when we truly make it our own. That is not easy. It would be much easier to forget, to ignore how the story we are weaving has two fewer hands bringing it into being with and sometimes through our own. If emptiness is the absence of horizons for what is relevant, the generic significance of the death of a loved one is to make us intensely aware—-for however briefly or long—-of the significance of everyone. Letters like yours are an occasion for me, a least, to become aware that each thing ramifies in all things, and that at some deep level we all are what we mean for one another."

I have read that suffering is the necessary deep feeling of the human situation. If we don't feel pain, suffering, human failure and weakness, we stand antiseptically apart from it and remain numb and small. We cannot understand such things by thinking about them. My own experience, unwanted as it is, has taught me that we understand only by living fully and openly what life put before us, experiencing and embodying each situation.

In living with trauma and grief over the death of my son I have learned the meaning of bearing witness to another's suffering. Bearing witness is more than a feeling evoking sympathy. Bearing witness is opening oneself to another's wounds. I have learned that the root *com* has to do with communion and *pan* in some languages is the word for bread and so I see that when we bear witness to another's pain we are in communion; breaking bread together. In bearing witness for another we walk along side the other, honoring the spirit, respecting disorder and confusion, being still, learning from others and remaining open and curious to life as it unfolds.

MEMORIES
Companion Poems
"It's a poor sort of memory that only works backward."
—Through the Looking Glass
by Lewis Carroll

The First Poem:
REMEMBERING

"He is very compassionate, caring,
especially concerned about other children
if they are hurt on the playground,
or if they are sad, especially the girls."
was the comment on my son's
progress report.
He was four.

"He created magic moments
for everyone who knew him,"
was a tribute voiced
by a city official
at my son,
The Mayor's,
memorial service.
He was forty.

CLARKSTON, GEORGIA
USA
January 22, 2011

The Second Poem:
REMEMBRANCES
(of a survivor)

He described it as primal fear:
the fear of a child
suddenly separated
from its mother.

In the smoke filled corridor
someone touched his arm
supporting him.

He said it felt like love.

He explained somehow
something of himself
dropped away.

Clinging to each other,
they found a path
to the stairwell.

He recalled his thoughts:
"Why don't we do this
all the time:
reach out with love
to guide each other."

Together they escaped
the First Tower.

NEW YORK CITY, NEW YORK
USA
September 11, 2001

Judy Beene Myers

IX

"The children, the children, I can't forget the children.

No matter where I go, I'll always see

those little faces looking up at me!"
—-Richard Rogers, The King and I

At this time the disciples came to Jesus and said, "Who is the greatest in the kingdom of Heaven. So he called a little child to him whom he set among them. The he said, 'In truth I tell you, unless you change and become like little children you will never enter the Kingdom of Heaven."
—-Matt. 18:1-4

I slowly open my eyes to the remaining darkness of early morning. The still branches outside my window are silhouetted against a soft lingering grey. In these moments just before first daylight pierces the sky, I hear their voices:
"I think the clock says 7. We can get up now, Beenie!" announces Alice Elizabeth, my 4-year- old granddaughter.
Immediately Ty, 3, bounds into our bedroom.
"Come here, Sugar Man!" I say.
"I not Sugar Man. I Ty."
He leaps into bed with us. I snuggle him close, silently thanking my son for their young lives. "You look like a Sugar Man. You feel like a Sugar Man. You taste like a Sugar Man. You must be a Sugar Man," I tease.
"I not a Sugar Man," he replies. "I Ty Tygrett!"
Now two days after Amy, my daughter-in-law, and my two young grandchildren have returned home and my

body has begun to rest back to what seems normal, the house is quiet: very quiet. I reflect on my summer of children. I reflect on my life filled with children and the exhausting joyfulness of being with them: my own children, their friends, my grandchildren and the many children I continue to work with.

When Trey was two years old, I began working with pre-schoolers at Highland Park Presbyterian Church Day School in Dallas, Texas A very good friend was teaching there and encouraged me to join her. I went to work for myself and for Trey. My son hit the floor running every day. His sister recently commented, "Trey did not miss much in the 40 years he was here. I would say he had a pretty full life!"

From the moment of birth, Trey faced life full of ener-gy. He made friends easily, was always thinking up a new project. Stubborn at times, but curious and eager, he thrust himself into each moment, never stopping until he reached the point of exhaustion.

His sister, Carroll, is 3 ½ years older. She began pre-school at age 3 and when she was away from home, Trey seemed lost and restless. Actually, we were both lost and restless without Carroll's presence, so working with children seemed the right thing for me. I could take my son with me to be in his own class while I taught. My hours coincided with my children's school hours and we all had holidays and summer vacations off together.

From this beginning, I continued through most of my children's growing up years working at various schools, usu-ally where one of them was attending. I have always found great pleasure in being with children of all ages. I helped with Trey's Cub Scout troop. I assisted in planning the Wil-derness Program while serving on the founding faculty of The Episcopal School of Dallas. Many summers Carroll, Trey and I went to day camps together where I worked as a counselor and they were campers or assistant counselors.

For most of my adult life, children, my own and others, have played a major role in my story.

In February following Trey's death I was notified by Tarrytown United Methodist Church Children's Day Out program that they needed an assistant one day a week for the spring semester. I immediately knew this was something I needed to do. I was aware also that working one day a week was all I could manage at the time. My grief had taught me not to expect too much of myself. My grief had taught me the importance of balancing my solitude with being in community.

I had taught in the program for seven years, beginning there just after we came to Austin, Texas. A year and a half earlier, I had resigned from fulltime employment and had continued substituting as needed. Still experiencing the rawness of the early period of my grief, I was cautious but certain this would be a safe place for me. I knew most of the teachers and assistants well and was confident I would be allowed the freedom to express myself openly and honestly without being questioned.

That spring I stayed close to the children and staff. I was not yet able to reach out in conversation to parents and grandparents. I was happy just to be there, quietly in the background. As soon as each school day ended, I left quickly out the back door. All I could do at the time was be present to the children and let them be present to me.

When children are given the opportunity to share from their hearts, beautiful things can happen. Right in the muck of my deepest grief, a lotus flower began to bloom. Beautiful things did happen for me in that classroom of one-and two-year-olds.

At naptime, I would lay on the floor beside, Campbell, a little girl who had difficulty settling down. She would sit straight up on her mat watching and waiting for me to take my place next to her. As we lay there side by side she looked at me with bright eyes, smiling while silently fingering my bracelet, touching my face and patting me. She was my comforter.

The following fall I returned to work full time. I continued on to participate in the summer session. I now plan to be there as long as I am able.

At the beginning of each school day, the teachers greet the children on the playground.

Many of them run happily to me. They love me. They often spontaneously tell me so. They laugh and dance with me. They sit with me in Silent Circles of Meditation I have developed inspired by Fr. Laurence Freeman's work with children in Christian Meditation. The school supportively allows me to lead four circles weekly for the 3- year-old classes.

After outdoor play, we come inside the classroom and take our places sitting cross legged in a circle around our little altar of heart shaped rocks. We light our candle and close our eyes. At the sound of three strikes of the prayer bowl, we sit silently remembering our hearts together.

"You have a strong voice," I tell them. "Everyone has a strong voice. It lives in your heart. It is the voice of kindness. You must be very still to hear it."

"Mine says I love my family," one says.

"Mine says to share," another adds.

"Mine says be nice," I hear a little voice say. I am reminded of Trey, "Mom, just be nice. Let's all be nice to each other."

Most children seem delightfully comfortable with the fact that life and death constantly exist side by side.

"Guess What!" a small boy said to me.

"Last week our dog went to heaven."

"Oh," I replied, "And how do you feel about that?"

"It's o.k." he said, "He was old. He feels better now. When I close my eyes, I see him. I can feel him next to me. Right here in my heart."

In her book *Blue Iris* Mary Oliver instructs us:

"Teach the children. We don't matter so much, but the children do. Show them daisies and the pale hepatica. Teach them the taste of sassafras and wintergreen. The lives of the blue sailors, mallow, sunbursts, the moccasin-flowers. And the frisky ones—- inkberry, lamb's-quarters, blueberries. And the aromatic ones—-rosemary, oregano. Give them the fields and the woods and the possibility of the world salvaged from the lords of profit. Stand them in the stream, head them upstream, rejoice as they learn to love this green space they live in, its sticks and leaves and then the silent, beautiful blossoms."

Each child I am privileged to be with is a petal of the blossom of Trey's new life within me. I see him in each young one I work with. I see him in his own two children who bring to me the smiles and laughter of their father, who ask me questions about him and eagerly listen to my answers. I see him in his sister, his wife and his niece and nephew, my other two grandchildren. I am reminded of his comments to me when Alice Elizabeth, his first child, was born,

"Mom, she is so tiny. Her foot fits in the palm of my hand!"

And when his son, Ty, arrived, Trey said beaming his outrageous grin,

"He's pretty cute, isn't he? They're going to have a lot of fun together."

They are all my children: my own, my husband's children and grandchildren, all the children I work with. They are all my blessings.

On the wall in the kitchen of a Zen Center I frequent hangs a saying,

"Open mind,

Loving mind,

Big mind,

Grandmother mind."

In Japanese *robai-shin* means Grandmother mind, the mind of great compassion. Zen Master Dogen taught the mind of great compassion is the mind of great empathy. This empathy helps all humanity. He says this mind is not developed from intelligence, ability or knowledge. I would say this mind is not developed: rather it be-comes in one. If nutured with silence and simplicity, Grandmother mind gradually comes into being from within one's soul.

I have experienced this mind in the minds of young children who are still so close to their origins that it seems to exhibit itself in their entire being. I am reminded of these verses in a John O'Donohue poem, As A Child Enters The World:

"In everything I do, think,

Feel, and say,

May I allow the light

Of the world I am leaving

To shine through and carry me home."

I have learned what Big Mind is telling me: The way is easy, just avoid picking and choosing. When you give up grasping and rejecting, the way unfolds before you. I am finding my way now by allowing the children to lovingly and joyfully carry me home.

THANKGIVING 2011

Children filled with boundless energy
joyously, lovingly greet the day,
each moment all there is.

The girl: masterful, curious,
with a sly certainty,
agile, quick,
meeting each challenge
independently confident.

The boy: teasingly assertive, clown-like,
running duck-feet across the sand,
chasing seagulls, sandpipers, side-stepping crabs.

clasping hands,
fleeing oncoming waves,
squeals of delight!

tropical blue-green ocean,
kites dancing on sea breezes,
seaweed, jellyfish, hermit crabs,
We catch and release.
scallop shells, windsurfers,
slow bikers, turtle refuge,
bay fishers, grandparents,
fried shrimp, po-boys, iced tea.

sand, sand, more sand,
starlight, big dipper,
north star, shooting star,
pelicans gliding,
sandpipers scurrying,
seagulls to be fed,
butterflies, dragonflies,
sea moss rose blossoms,
pink sunrise, orange sunset.

three generations, family,
sunburn, tired bones,
memories, memories, memories,

acceptance, acceptance, acceptance
gratitude, gratitude, gratitude
—-Judy Beene Myers

X

"I have a feeling that my boat

has struck, down there in the depths,

against a great thing.

And nothing happens!

Nothing. Silence. Waves,

—-nothing happens.

Or has everything happened?

And we are standing now,

quietly, in the new life."
—Juan Ramon Jimenez

The Well of Grief

Those who will not slip beneath

the still surface on the well of grief

turning downward through its black water

to the place we cannot breathe

will never know the source from which we drink

the secret water, cold and clear,

nor find in the darkness of glimmering

The small round coins

thrown by someone who wished for something else.

—David Whyte

On the first day of the retreat in Taos, I sat alone with my teacher. As I faced him with tears streaming down my cheeks he asked, "What can we do to help you?"

"Just do what you and everyone is doing," I answered, "Just be here."

I did not know if I could be helped. I did not know what I felt except that I was sinking. I was drowning. I had come to the well of grief. I had slipped beneath its waters. Some part of me wanted to say, "Please bring me a large bowl of warm, salty water. I want to put my face in it. I want to hold my breath and lay my face in warm, tender, soft caressing water. I want to sense its refreshing touch of renewal. I want to know it is holding me and that even if my face sinks down to touch the bottom, the water's buoyancy will lift me once again to the surface and I will raise my head and breathe."

I did not make this request at that moment for fear of sounding crazy. Now I know that grief renders one crazy at times. There is no ordinary or usual way of doing anything. There is no logical sense to what grief asks of one when in the depths of experiencing its powerful emotions.

I embraced Jimenez's words with relief for expressing my anguish. I felt my boat had struck in the depths; a great thing and nothing and everything was happening. I did not feel I was standing quietly in the new life. I felt I wanted to be submerged in, comforted and renewed by the presence and power of water.

Our bodies are more than 60% water and water covers approximately 70% of the planet. Maybe I was seeking reconnection to myself, reconnection to life, reconnection to connection. I wanted to dive deep into the silence and find shining beneath its waves the hidden treasure of everlasting hope.

There in that reconnection I wanted to feel the presence of my son, the presence of life, "We are connected. All the water here on Earth now is all the water there ever was, and ever will be. Through the cycling of water, across space and time, we are linked to all of life.—-Earth's water, embedded with the wisdom of the ages, is literally in our blood. And as molecules of water circulate from sea to air to land—-through the clouds, through the rivers, through the trees, through the frogs and fish and mussels and beetles and ants and birds and bees and everything alive, now and then and yet to be—-we are connected." So writes Sandra Postel in Honest Hope.

In those early months after Trey's death, I was so broken and fragile. I wanted to be held by everything. Memories of sunset on January 1, 2011, sometimes flooded back upon me. I experienced again wading into the cold Gulf waters on the shores of South Padre Island to put my son's ashes in the sea.

I cannot remember planning the event. Perhaps Amy planned it. Perhaps she was the one who should have planned it. I do not know if there is a protocol for planning a memorial service in the face of such an unexpected and tragic loss. I cannot remember much prior to the event. I just remember it happened. I knew when and where it would take place. It seemed to me the right thing to do: to return my son to the elements of life from which he had received his being.

When I think of my life and the lives of my children, I will always remember the sea. We spent so many summers playing on the beach together. I see us again race across hot sand to secure an ocean-cooled spot at the edge of the surf for beach towels, umbrellas and all the necessary gear children insist on bringing along for play.

Fearless and sure of himself Trey always bounded out into the waves before I knew it.

"Trey, you're going out too far!" I would call to him.

"I'm o.k. don't worry, Mom," he would laugh back.

On many occasions he expressed his hope to someday live near the sea.

In June following Trey's death, I returned to the Hawaiian Islands for the first time in six years at which time we put my mother's ashes in the Pacific Ocean off the coast of Kauai. This time I traveled to the island of Molokai where, with my intimate friend and guide, I immersed myself in familiar waters, an ocean of Aloha. I found comfort and healing there. I felt a homecoming.

As I dove deep into the sea, I dropped beneath the surface of what seemed to be happening into the depths of what I knew and know is real. It was the beginning of allowing a process beyond my limited mind to work through me. I began to know for certain a new life would emerge.

"Nothing of him that doth fade,

But doth suffer as a sea-change

Into something rich and strange."
—Shakespeare, The Tempest

My family has had an ongoing relationship with Hawaii, particularly Kauai, beginning with my grandparents who visited there for the first time in the 1950s. For years, my mother returned annually for lengthy stays at her island home, situated on a cliff overlooking the clear, tropical emerald ocean.

My children were very young when we first began our visits there. Many island mornings we would hurry down the long winding path to the base of the cliff, climb over lava rocks, hurry across the dark, coarse volcanic sand and plunge delightedly into the ocean's arms.

Together we hiked through cane fields with native families to the hidden slippery slide to slip down the natural rock slide and drop into the depths of a deep, clear rainforest pool. Each time my children took the plunge, I held my breath, awaiting the sight of their curly heads breaking the water's surface and hearing their voices call out to me, "Again, again. Can we do it again? Please, please, again!"

Kauai, the oldest of the Hawaiian island chain, was born of the sea in a volcanic eruption arising from its depths many centuries ago. Since my first visit there, I have felt deeply connected to the Aloha spirit, which cannot be explained. It can only be experienced.

During her months on the mainland, my mother would often say,

"Honey, I hear the islands calling me." My children and I sensed the same familiar call. This sense of the call of the island, the call of the sea has on many occasions during the past year and a half brought me back to life. Even now, though these periods of grief occur less frequently, I sometimes unexpectedly find myself swept to the depths of despair in a now familiar tsunami of sorrow.

Recently, prior to resuming the school year, I was scheduled to meet with the other teachers for a morning session to renew our CPR certification. It was our first day back together for the new school year. I had no idea until I walked into the room, signed in with the instructor and sat down at the table, how instantly everything would flash back. I had to leave the room. I had to ask to be excused from the session.

I needed time to let the memories of those early Christmas morning hours, real and imagined, flow back in and through me. I could hear their voices again; members of Amy's family explaining what had happened. They told me of Amy's nephew administering CPR to Trey faithfully and continually until the EMS arrived. Again in the silent, deep interior of the waters of despair, it seems as always happens I reached a point when my struggle for the breath of life forced me back to the surface until again I broke through the waves and out into the sunlight.

Artist of the ocean Ran Orther says, "You do not mess with the ocean. It will pummel you and chew you up. It is devastatingly brutal. And yet it can be luminous and delicate and tender. We clean our wounds there."

I have learned from grief counselors that experiencing natural elements are healing to trauma victims. While I may find healing in water, particularly the ocean, another might find comfort in working with the soil or walking in the woods. One way or another to live life fully again the griever must find a way to clean the wounds of grief. I could amend Orhter's quote to say, "You do not mess with grief. It will pummel you and chew you up. It is devastatingly brutal.

And yet it can be luminous and delicate and tender. We clean our wounds when facing our grief."

Grief teaches us true humility. Some call it "radical humility," for in facing grief, one glimpses and comes to accept the Mystery. One does not seek the intense experience of grief, but each one of us sometime in life is brought to the edge, sometimes without warning, and falls into it. I depend totally on the love and support that surrounds me and yet I know completely that this is my path alone. In my aloneness I am held together by community.

This past summer, my husband and I rented a condo on Padre Island, where we spent a week with Alice Elizabeth and Ty and my daughter, Carroll. We played together in the ocean, the ocean of my ancestors' ashes, the ocean of my son's ashes. It was a peaceful, playful time of family community. Together and individually we experienced healing. I felt that sense of peace and knowing, "we are standing now, quietly, in the new life."

IN THE BEGINNING

In the beginning was today.

Morning vapors rolled

silently into the valleys,

obscuring hills,

clinging to tree limbs,

droplets sparkling,

crystal beaded, jeweled accents

landing on spider webs.

The earth's pulse throbbed

into my soul,

the breath of God

breathed into me

and I was given life.

—-Judy Beene Myers; Mount Calvary, September 2008

XI

Overcome any bitterness that may have come

because you were not up to the magnitude of the pain

that was entrusted to you.

Like the Mother of the world

who carries the pain of the world in her heart,

each one of us is part of her heart,

and therefore endowed

with a certain measure of cosmic pain.

You are sharing in the totality of that pain.

You are called upon to meet it in joy

instead of self-pity.
—Sufi saying

Mothers who have lost children are the standard-bearers for carrying the pain of the world. As the saying states, we are each part of the heart of the Mother of the World and each are sharing the totality of that pain. Our challenge is to meet that pain with joy.

In what seems to be the natural order of the death of our loved ones, we expect to lose parents, perhaps a spouse, maybe a sibling, but never do we expect to lose a child. However, somewhere in the deep recesses of a mother's anxiousness lies her greatest fear: the fear of the death of her child: and yet she never expects that to happen.

There is that word again—-*never*. This should *never* happen, but it did. He is *never* coming back. I will *never* be the same. No, I will *never* be the same, but as I allow my heart to break open as Parker Palmer said, rather than remaining shattered, something vaster than either Trey or me is allowed to emerge. So what will *never* be again gives way for something new to be born and therein joy is discovered.

During this process of integrating the loss of my son into my life, I have been supported at My Healing Place, a non-profit grief center here in Austin, by other parents of children who have died. I have found acceptance, understanding, safety, connectedness and compassion through participating in sharing stories with other grieving mothers and fathers.

My group consists of parents of varying ages and different socio-economic, educational and religious backgrounds. Like a mini Clarkston, Georgia, the town Trey served as mayor, we are a diverse community of refugees seeking acceptance, understanding and hope. With all our differences we are brought together in the commonality of our grief. We share our sense of heartfelt loss, confusion and brokenness. Together we learn to face the pain "*in joy instead of self-pity.*" We begin again to accept our lives as they are now and move into becoming present to its flow.

Through these encounters my life has become more precious, more focused, more intentional. I walk more humbly and meet the days more openly and gratefully. I am reminded that little is required of me other than

"To act justly,

to love tenderly

and to walk humbly with my God." Micah 6:8

For years I have kept readily available to myself a particular poem. Copies can be found on my desk or in my famous "stacks of stuff," as my family calls what I consider very important papers. Occasionally I discover a copy randomly stuck in a book, usually just when I need it. I have learned I must be constantly reminded of who I truly am and where I am going. "The Way It Is" by William Stafford always helps keep me on track.

"There's a thread you follow. It goes among

things that change. But it doesn't change.

People wonder about what you are pursuing.

You have to explain about the thread.

But it is hard for others to see.

While you hold it you can't get lost.

Tragedies happen; people get hurt

or die; and you suffer and get old.

Nothing you do can stop time's unfolding.

You don't ever let go of the thread."

The thread I follow has led me to people and communities I have been able to openly and comfortably rely on for acceptance and love. I have willingly entered fully into these encounters of presence. I know if I am to live the life I have remaining completely and freely in the face of this tragic event, I have no other choice. To honor Trey, to honor the great web of life itself of which I am a part, I continue to follow my thread. I have and am led into an ever-widening circle of connection. The words "no separation" are no longer just words offering limited reasonable understanding. The words "no separation" have become who I am.

The tiny seed of awareness of how limitless are our connections to all of life began to take root within me when I entered Amy's parents' home Christmas afternoon 2010. There before me were members of Amy's blended family, some of whom I had never met, who had been present for my son's last evening of life and his death. We were now brought together as family and strangers witnessing each other's shock and sorrow.

In the week that followed, we were joined by other friends and family members. A month later in Clarkston, Georgia, I honored Trey's life with the refugee community, state and local officials, coworkers from REI, former classmates and faculty members from The Webb School, and many of his childhood friends.

Through these relationships I slowly began to realize how the life of each person affected by my son's life and his death flows out into the universe like an ever widening ripple on a stream endlessly flowing through the lives of countless others. I began to sense the true meaning of "no separation." The influence of one life on each of our lives is mysteriously connected to and affects all of life. Clearly, every choice each of us makes is immeasurable and profoundly significant.

When death occurs, when someone or some circumstance in one's life drops away, an opening is left for something new to emerge. I believe we each have a role in co-creating with the mystery of creation something fresh, vibrant, grand and full of wonder. Eight months after Trey's death I was asked to be in a writing group. During those first few sessions and for the first six months, I was unable to do any more than just show up.

I remember when I first came into AA over 26 years ago, they told me, "just don't take a drink and get to a daily meeting." They said, "just keep coming back. It will get better. You'll always be an alcoholic but you don't have to drink."

It is the same with grief. Those who guided me said, "it will get better. You will always be the mother of a son who died but your life has not ceased. You will learn to integrate this loss into your life. You will see the light again."

It is the same with the writing group. I was encouraged to keep coming back. Something within me told me, "just show up even if you say nothing, even if you write nothing: just be there."

Eventually I did begin to say something. Eventually I did begin to write. From a small beginning, I wrote more and more. I began to give myself through my writing to others. I continue to write as my offering to whomever might benefit from my experience as a gift in gratitude for my son's life.

As stories of others in the writing group have come forth, my awareness of "no-separation" has been validated. One story in particular has brought forth joy in the midst of my grief:

On Christmas Eve 2010, Trey's last evening on earth, as one life was soon to end another was beginning anew. That same night 10-month-old Josephine, an Ethiopian orphan, arrived with her new parents at their home here in Austin, and a family was born. Simultaneously, somewhere in Ethiopia another mother was grieving, perhaps alone, the loss of that child.

I see that love and grief, joy and sorrow forever exist side by side. As the story of the adoption of Josephine, this Ethiopian child, unfolded, I discovered that in truth we walk on parallel paths with many companions. Only by sharing stories are our connections revealed.

John O'Donohue says we grieve for ourselves, not for the one who is gone. The one who has gone is at peace. As months have passed since Trey's death, I grieve for myself less often. A space from the center of my being is opening for my son to become alive in new ways that allow his presence constantly to be with me.

I have room now to grieve for that Ethiopian mother, who perhaps had no one to grieve with, no time to grieve. I have room to grieve for the world.

At the same time I am joyful: joyful that I have two healthy, happy grandchildren and a caring daughter-in-law living just a half-day drive away. I am joyful for a husband and wife who until December 25, 2010, were just a couple, and by welcoming and adopting an orphaned child have created a family. I am joyful for a mother half a world away who let go, knowing she was sending her child into a better life. I am joyful that my husband at 82 is healthy, still able to teach swimming and has had the privilege of teaching Josephine to swim. I am joyful that our lives have intertwined in the unending circle of life.

"When you love, you always risk pain. The more deeply you love, the greater the risk that you will be hurt. Yet to live your life without loving is not to have lived at all. As deeply as you open to life, so deeply will life open to you. So there is a lovely symmetry and proportion between grief and love." says John O'Donohue. In finding this lovely symmetry and proportion, I am finding my way beyond just the memory of Trey's life. I am allowing his life to be forever woven into the tapestry of mine.

XII

"You sent out beyond your recall,

go to the limits of your longing.

Embody me.

Flare up like flame

and make big shadows I can move in.

Let everything happen to you: beauty and terror.

Just keep going. No feeling is final.

Don't let yourself lose me.

Give me your hand.
—-Rilke, Book of Hours.

"In your light I learn how to love.

In your beauty, how to make poems.

You dance inside my chest,

Where no one sees you,

But sometimes I do, and that

Sight becomes this art."
—Rumi

"God is love. In love we give and in the giving we find ourselves in the other."
— Fr. Laurence Freeman

"Our aspiration, our calling, our desire for a genuine life, is to see the truth of who we really are—-that the nature of our Being is connectedness and love, not the illusion of a separate self to which our suffering clings. It is from this awareness that Life can flow through us; The Unconditioned manifesting freely as our conditioned body."
—-Ezra Bayda

This is a love story. It is not what one might think of in the usual sense of the word. There is not necessarily a happy ending. Perhaps there is and at the same time there is not. It is a story that moves beyond happy endings, as it has no beginning and no end. It is a story that simply is and was and ever more shall be.

This is a love story of suffering, joy, hope and light. I have found in the process of writing this story that in truth, love is much vaster than a feeling. Love is who we are. We were created by love, are forever held in love and when we return to the Presence, the Source of all being, we will discover it is simply this wonder of love. Our love for ourselves and others is made manifest through how we chose to meet our suffering.

I have also discovered while writing this story a clearer understanding of the meaning of unconditional love, which I understand as Mark Nepo explains it, "Unconditional love is not so much about how we receive and endure each other, as it is about the deep vow to never, under any condition, stop bringing the flawed truth of who we are to each other."

The flawed truth of who I am lies in my humanness. My humanness has been totally revealed as the result of my grief. There are times I am so overcome by sorrow, so in need of opening this well of grief in the presence of others that I have no choice other than to allow myself to be exposed like a slain animal lying slashed open in the field, helplessly waiting for whatever comes, vulture or healer. I have experienced both. I have felt what was once the warmth of familiar friends become cold, distant and silent.

Wendell Berry says, "It's our separatedness and grief that breaks the world in two."On the other hand, strangers have welcomed me with open hearts and listening ears."I was a stranger and you made me welcome." Matt. 25:36

A few months ago I attended a lecture given by one of my teachers. He began by saying, "I thought for some time about what to talk about tonight, trying to consider what this audience would like to hear. Finally, I put everything aside and decided I would talk about what I felt so I am going to talk about love."

If I never remember more than his opening statement, I hope to remember, as I live with this unending yet transforming grief, to put everything else aside and allow my life to be what it already is: simply love.

We were born for love and connection. Our lives depend on it. When my children came into the world, they evoked my deepest love, my deepest sense of connection. I have read that under the right circumstances we are able to remember our own births.

We can recall that feeling of the process being too difficult. We resisted being born into the world. We wanted to remain in the place of warmth, comfort and safety.

So it is with facing grief and allowing it to become transformative. Richard Rohr says that pain that is not transformed is transferred. This is revealed in the awareness that so many people inflict pain on others because of their own pain. So as in any war, war within myself will result in collateral damage for others in my life, probably more far reaching that I can imagine. Under no circumstance and in spite of all the sorrow, anger and confusion I must face, can I allow that to happen.

There are unexpected moments when I want to leap up, rush out the door, run down the street and catch my boy. I want to stop it all. At times I feel the pain will never cease. Now as I write and the seasons have made the turn toward the second Christmas since he died, I begin to sense some sort of underlying dread. Still, I hold on to this love so deep within with assurance that it has and will never let me go.

"Here is the thing, say Shug: The thing I believe. God is inside you and inside everybody else. You come into the world with God. But only them that search for it inside find it. And sometimes it just manifest itself even if you not looking, or don't know what you're looking for. Trouble do it for most folKs, I think. Sorrow, Lord."
—-Alice Walker, The Color of Purple

In loving deeply, we must acknowledge that with each love there will come a time of farewell. Our most intimate loves surely produce the most difficult and painful farewells.

We let go of the beloved with displays of raging intimacy, kindled by fires of anger brought forth from the depths of that love. We say farewell to what once was manifest here in the physical presence of that love, then fall to our knees in the nakedness of surrender to receive the immense vastness of eternal, everlasting love. To live fully there is no other way.

"If you asked me what I came to do in this world—-I came to live out loud."
—-Emile Zola

This is what Trey came into the world to do and this is what he did. He lived out loud. The first three months of his life he could not sleep at night. The only way I was able to rest myself was to lie on the living room couch with his tiny body nesting on mine. To the slow, quiet rhythms of our heart beats and breath, we lulled each other to sleep.

For Trey's fifth birthday I impulsively bought him a bike without training wheels. He could not wait to try it out. I steadied him, ran along beside him, then let go. Once, twice, three times and he was off with joyous assurance; a boy on a bike eagerly headed toward the adventure called life.

Trey never knew a stranger. His enthusiasm radiated. Having once latched on to an idea, there was absolutely no stopping him sometimes to the total frustration of his dad, his sister and me. He introduced many people to the things he loved best: kayaking, hiking, rappelling, playing the guitar. We shared a love of the music of such poets as Bob Dylan and Neil Young. As soon as she could walk, Alice Elizabeth twirled to her daddy's foot stomping guitar tunes. A favorite was and always will be "Harvest Moon."

"Come a little bit closer,

hear what I have to say.

Just like children sleepin'

we could dream this night away.

But there's a full moon risin'

let's go dancin' in the light.

We know where the musics playin'

let's go out and feel the light.

Because I'm still in love with you,

I want to see you dance again

—on this Harvest moon."
—Neil Young

Trey love to surprise the people in his life. He arranged to have the whole family and his best friend, Tony, present for a Fourth of July celebration in Austin so he could propose to Amy in the delighted presence of us all.

I remember Trey's hands. In my memories I recall the hands of those who have been closest to me, those who have nurtured me, not just with words, but with their hands. We need to touch each other. We need to touch each other often. Our hands can be our outward expression of our love for others. Our hands are an extension of our hearts. When hands and hearts work together we are able to reach right into a person, holding them, supporting them from within. I do not mean just a casual, habitual hug, I mean a heart-hand touch of assurance. There is a difference. We Americans need to learn the difference. We need to learn that our hands are for more than busy-ness; they are for touching each other, holding each other and for expressing our deepest love.

Trey had big bear hands, strong and at the same time tender. During these months since his death, I have seen his hands through the eyes of my memories and dreams. I vividly remember the last time I hugged him goodbye, the last time our hands touched.

Love has revealed itself to me in many new and unexpected ways in the months since my son's death. At Mayfield Park I walk down the wooded trail, cross the stream and climb to the top of a rocky ledge somewhat hidden in the woods. I call it my healing rock. I sit and reflect on this new phase of my life. With gratitude I remember all the love I have received and that continues to flow through family, friends, experiences in the natural world and in my solitude. I cannot go back. I can only look forward to the life that I have yet to live here. Some days are more painful than others, but there is much, much joy revealed to me continually in many unexpected ways. I try to remain open and aware and to constantly walk holding both grief and joy. I am grateful: grateful for life itself and for my deep awareness that everything is always right here right now.

"When I, a student of the way,

look at the real form of the universe,

all is the never-failing manifestation

of the mysterious truth of the awakened life.

In any event, in any moment, and in any place,

none can be other than the marvelous revelation

of its glorious light."
—-Bodhisattva's Vow

"Jesus said: I am the light above everything. I

am everything. Everything came forth from

me, and everything reached me.

Split wood, I am here. Lift up a rock, you

will find me there."
—The Gospel of Thomas, 77a, 77b

God is in everything, even this right here, right now: just as God is in Trey, in me, in everyone, in every living thing, in every event, in all that exists. Everything is alive and everything is alive with, in and through God. World without end. Amen

Author's Note

On December 24, 2012 Ed and I and my daughter, Carroll, joined Amy's family in toasting Christmas and family before we sat down to Christmas Eve dinner. We were there together in the place where Trey died two years previously. We were there celebrating joyously the season and our togetherness as family.

I shared a recollection:

My grandson, Jack, now 10 years old, as a toddler, would often sing from the backseat of the car,

"Father Abraham had many sons,

many sons had Father Abraham.

I am one of them and so are you......"

Pause—-silence—-then,

"Beenie [the name my grandchildren and all children call me], that must mean we are all family; all of us on earth!"
"I would say so," I would reply. Then he would continue the song,
"So let's all praise the Lord!"
In Hawaiian the word for family is ohana. My granddaughter, Ginger, who loves animated films, pointed out to me one day that Lilo explains in the movie, "Lilo and Stitch," that ohana, family, means "nobody gets left behind. Or forgotten."

"Yes," I said. "Those who have gone before us are always with us. And even those that sometimes we feel we don't like—-they are still our family.

So there we all were, Christmas 2012, brought together from many places by many different circumstances; rejoicing with those present and remembering those absent celebrating the birth of Jesus, the promise of Abraham, with and in the presence of love.

With heartfelt gratitude for their love and support on my journey and through this project to: Jolynn Free, Flint Sparks and Peg Syverson and to Patty Speier, Director of Seton Cove in Austin, who has led me so many enriching resources for spiritual growth, who told me for many years, "You need to write. You have so much to say," and who held my head in her lap that tragic Christmas morning and of course, to my ever loving and always encouraging husband, Ed

I also want to thank my copy editor, Gerald Tilma, Assistant Director of the Undergraduate Writing Center at The University of Texas, one of the unexpected gifts to me on this journey ,and to my friend, Julie Ballard, who has graciously shared her family with me through the years, for saying "yes" to my request for her assistance in proof reading.

TAOS
Two Years Later

I am wondering if death
might be like this:
Having such a weariness overtake me
while walking in a snowfall toward home,
my arms and legs so heavy
they seem useless, cumbersome, in fact.

The coat on my back weights me down
until I remove it,
then stop to sit on a bench
and rest
hoping to catch my breath.

I look toward the mountain.
The storm is moving in.
A dark grey cloud hangs on its rim.
Snowflakes twirl.
Beyond the turmoil in the distance
perhaps arising from the desert floor
I see a glimpse of sunlight.
Its mysterious airiness
seems to steer
the dark cloud forward.

I arise from my resting place,
wrap the coat around my shoulders
and begin again to walk the path
toward home

Judy Beene Myers
February 2013

Contacts: Trey
404-963-5819

"Can call him?
I want to talk to him. I miss my daddy."
Confident her grandmother could make
anything happen,
she asked with a child's delighted anticipation.

Her daddy, my son,
dead now more than two years
remains forever part of us.

Seed of my seed, seed of his seed,
the two of us connected
in this Trinitarian triangle
by one whose essence lives within our hearts.

I pondered momentarily, then answered,
"This is not all there is, you know.
One night I spoke with him..
He called to tell me he was fine,
that he must be where he is now.

"Tell everyone I'm good," he said,
I can do so much for all of you form here."

Was I dreaming? What is a dream?
At times, perhaps, an unexpected gift of mercy.

"Close your eyes, my child, be still.
Be sure that you can call him
any time you wish.
He will always answer.
You will hear him in the beat of life itself,
in all you feel and think and do.
His voice will be eternally
resounding in your soul.

To: Alice Elizabeth Tygrett
From: Beenie"
March 2013

Made in the USA
Charleston, SC
19 June 2013